MISSION SURVIVAL:
SAVING EARTH'S ENDANGERED ANIMALS



# SAVING THE CHIMPANZEE

KATHERINE EASON

CHERITON
CHILDREN'S BOOKS

Published in 2026 by **Cheriton Children's Books**
1 Bank Drive West, Shrewsbury, Shropshire SY3 9DJ, UK



First Edition

Author: Katherine Eason
Designer: Paul Myerscough
Editor: Jane Brooke
Proofreader: Ella Newby
Consultant: David Hawksett, BSc

Picture credits: Cover: Flickr/Tambako the Jaguar. Inside: pp4-5: Shutterstock/Jane Rix, p6: Shutterstock/Eric Isselee, p7: Shutterstock/Sharon Morris, p8: Shutterstock/Robert Harding Video, p9: Shutterstock/Jane Rix, p11: Wikimedia Commons/Giles Laurent, p12b: Shutterstock/Sergey Uryadnikov, p12t: Shutterstock/Martin Pelanek, p13b: Shutterstock/Jane Rix, p13t: Shutterstock/Mark Higgins, pp14-15: Shutterstock/AlvaroGO, pp16-17: Shutterstock/Jane Rix, p17b: Shutterstock/Evgeny Bakharev, p17c: Shutterstock/Evgeny Bakharev, pp18-19: Shutterstock/Nokuro, p19b: Shutterstock/Nick Greaves, p20: Shutterstock/Roger de la Harpe, p21b: Shutterstock/Yakcuteboy, p21t: Shutterstock/Tau5, pp22-23: Shutterstock/Phil Hyde, p23b: Shutterstock/Tutatamafilm, p23c: Shutterstock/Tutatamafilm, pp24-25: Shutterstock/Gerdie Hutomo, p24b: Shutterstock/MattiaATH, p26: Shutterstock/Nick Biemans, p27b: Shutterstock/Wirestock Creators, p27c: Shutterstock/Wirestock Creators, p27t: Shutterstock/Dennis Jacobsen, pp28-29: Shutterstock/Kiki Dohmeier, p28b: Shutterstock/Nyxen Arch, p29c: Shutterstock/Asier Romero, p29t: Shutterstock/Asier Romero, pp30-31: Shutterstock/Martin Prochazkacz, p31t: Shutterstock/Elen Marlen, p32: Wikimedia Commons/Giles Laurent, p33b: Shutterstock/Sergey Uryadnikov, p33c: Shutterstock/LiaoZhuangDjiu, p33t: Shutterstock/Tukio, pp34-35: Shutterstock/CherylRamalho, p34b: Shutterstock/Sianc, p34c: Shutterstock/Sianc, pp36-37: Shutterstock/Meawpong3405, p36b: Shutterstock/Neurobit, pp38-39: Shutterstock/Nicole Piepgras, p39b: Shutterstock/Wirestock Creators, p39c: Shutterstock/TajdidProtik, pp40-41: Shutterstock/Crystal Alba, p40b: Shutterstock/Krakenimages.com, p40c: Shutterstock/Krakenimages.com, p42: Shutterstock/Boonchoke, p43: Shutterstock/Michaela Pilch, p44: Shutterstock/Sergey Uryadnikov, p45: Shutterstock/Jane Rix.



Printed in China

Publisher's Note: The information in the Kids on a Mission features in this book are suggestions for actions that children can take to help protect endangered animals, based on extensive research by the author and consultant. The email addresses and the children featured in the photographs are for illustrative purposes only.

# CONTENTS

# CHIMPS IN DANGER

Chimps are one of our closest living **relatives**. They are similar to humans in many ways. Chimps are highly intelligent and emotional animals. They live in groups and have important relationships within those groups. Sadly, because of humans, there is a danger that these remarkable animals may become extinct, or die out.

## IN DANGER AND DISAPPEARING

Chimps have been decreasing in numbers for decades. That is because of human actions. Adult chimps are hunted and killed by humans for their meat. Their babies are sold as pets or for entertainment. People take over chimps' land to make space for farming and logging, which is the cutting down of trees for wood. They also build homes on areas where chimps live. As humans take over more land, the animals lose their homes, food, and water. When hungry chimps then look for food on farms, they may come into contact with people. That can result in conflict, or physical clashes, in which chimps are harmed or killed. Chimps can also catch human diseases and die.

Chimps are under threat, but there is still time to save these incredible creatures. ▶

## CHIMPS GONE FOREVER?

All these challenging changes to their **environment** are making it harder for chimps to find food, water, and suitable places to live. Humans are pushing chimps into extinction. **Conservationists** are warning us that we need to do more to save the remaining chimps on Earth. The threats to chimps are real, and if we do not do something, one day they may be gone forever.

## HELP THE CHIMP!

There is still hope for the chimp, and it is not too late to save it. People everywhere have heard the chimp's call for help. And they are making it their mission to help these amazing animals survive. In this book, we'll learn about the chimp and why it is in danger. We'll discover what people are doing to help chimps and how they have built a career in **conservation**. We'll find out how kids everywhere can make it their mission to help save the chimp. And we'll learn how you could make a career in conservation your mission. Feeling mission-ready? Then read on!

*"The more we learn about chimpanzees, the more we realize that they are not just like us, but they are us—our closest living relatives."*

Jane Goodall, **primatologist** and conservationist

The International Union for Conservation of Nature (IUCN) keeps a record of the world's **species** and how at risk of **extinction** they are. It is called the **Red List.**

There are more than **46,000** animal species on the List.

The chimp is listed as **endangered.**

CHAPTER ONE

# MEET THE CHIMP

Chimps are known as one of man's closest relatives. This is because they share 98 to 99 percent of their **DNA** with humans. Chimp bodies are similar to those of humans. They also behave like humans in many ways.

### HUMANLIKE HANDS

Like us, chimps have ten fingers on their humanlike hands and ten toes on their feet. Chimps' hands and feet have **opposable** fingers and thumbs, like a human hand. This allows them to grasp branches and food. The hands of a chimp can perform delicate movements, allowing the animal to **manipulate** tools with great skill.

## TIP TO TOE

Chimps' bodies are a similar size and shape to ours, but they have longer arms and shorter legs than humans. Their bodies are covered in dark-brown-to-black hair. Only their palms, soles of their feet, and face are hairless.

## WALKING TALL

Chimps sometimes stand up and walk on their back legs, like humans, but usually walk on all fours. Adult chimps are up to 5.5 feet (1.7 m) tall when standing upright. That's the height of an average adult man. Adult male chimps weigh up to 132 pounds (60 kg). Females are smaller, weighing up to 110 pounds (50 kg).

## FACES THAT TALK

Chimps have large, **expressive** eyes and lips. These features allow the animals to make a wide range of **facial expressions**. These facial movements are very important as they help chimps **communicate** with their group. Chimps also use sounds, body language, and **gestures** to show their thoughts and feelings.

# In a Group

**Scientists group animals to help classify, or order, them. Chimps belong to a species of animals called *Pan troglodytes*. The species is divided into four subspecies. The subspecies are the Western chimpanzee, the Central chimpanzee, the Eastern chimpanzee, and the Nigeria-Cameroon chimpanzee.**

# WHERE CHIMPS LIVE

Chimps live in Africa. They live in hot and wet **lowland forests**, **swamp forests**, and **montane forests**. They are also found in dry forests, **savanna woodlands**, and farmland. The land on which chimps live has been reduced as the human **population** has grown. As more people have moved on to chimp land, that has forced animals out of the places in which they live. Chimps have lost about half of their land since the 1960s.

## FOUND ACROSS AFRICA

The different subspecies of chimps live in different areas of Africa.

- Western chimps live in dry and **humid** lowland forests, open savannas, and woodlands of West Africa. They are also found in land cleared for **oil palm plantations**.
- Central chimps are found in the lush **rain forests** of the Congo Basin in central Africa.
- Eastern chimps live in the humid lowland forests, cooler submontane forests, and savanna woodlands in Eastern Africa.
- Nigeria-Cameroon chimps are found in the humid lowland forests, montane and submontane forests. They also live in dry forest, savanna woodland, and farmland along the border of Nigeria and Cameroon in Central and West Africa.

Chimps walk with their knuckles (not their palms) ▶ touching the ground. This helps them balance and keeps their hands free for gathering food.

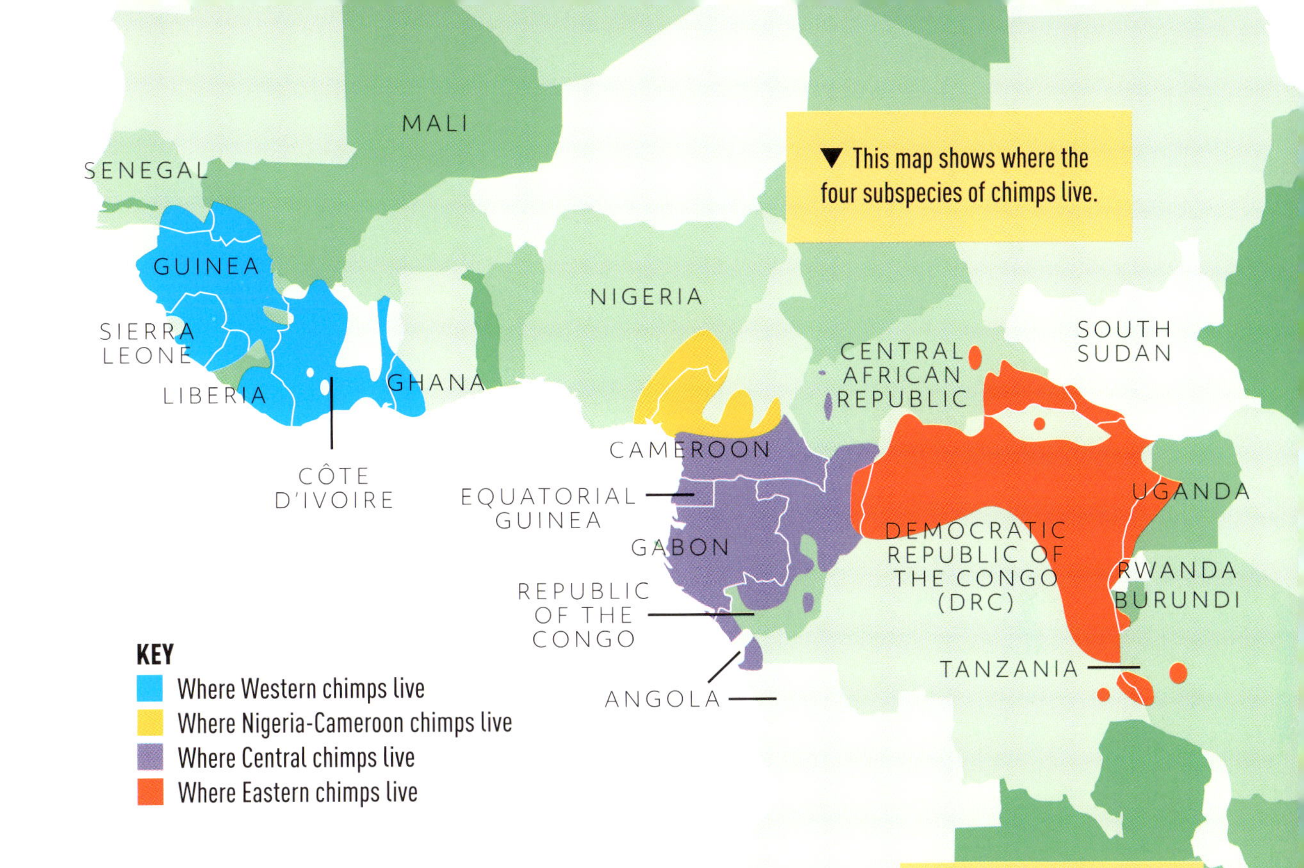


▼ This map shows where the four subspecies of chimps live.

## LIVING UNDER THREAT

Western chimps are the most threatened subspecies of chimp and are considered **critically endangered**. Large areas of their **habitat** have been cleared for farmland, logging, and human homes. There are fewer than 9,000 Nigeria-Cameroon chimps left. The spread of humans and threat from **poaching** has forced these chimps into small, broken-up areas of montane rain forest. Central and Eastern chimps' homes are also under threat from human activities such as home building, logging, **mining**, and farming. As chimps lose their land, it becomes more difficult for them to find food, water, and forests in which to live.

▼ Chimps hoot to communicate with each other across large distances. This Eastern chimpanzee lives in Kibale National Park, western Uganda. This is a protected area in which chimps can live more safely.

# WHY SHOULD WE HELP THE CHIMP?

Chimps are not only incredibly intelligent animals, but they are also very important to the environments in which they live. They help to keep their habitats healthy. Without chimps, the places in which they live would suffer.

## CONTROLLING PLANTS AND ANIMALS

Chimps eat a lot of fruit and swallow the seeds inside the fruit. The seeds pass through the chimp's **digestive system** whole and come out later in their waste. Because chimps move around a lot, the seeds are dropped far from the trees they grew on. They grow into new plants and trees, providing food and shelter for chimps. Along with eating plants, chimps also hunt other animals for meat. This keeps the number of animals in the forest in check.

## IMPORTANT FOR US ALL

Protecting chimps' habitats helps chimps, and all the plants and animals that live there. It also helps people. The forests where chimps live are important for controlling Earth's climate. They also provide people with food and medicines.

Chimps play a very ▶ important role in their ecosystem.

## CLOSE RELATIVES

Chimps are one of our closest relatives. Studying chimps helps us understand how human intelligence, social behavior, and language developed. Chimps are incredibly intelligent and emotional animals. Like humans, chimps have close friendships and show each other kindness. They comfort friends and family when they are upset and help other chimps in need. They share and play with their friends and family and make up after fights. We share so many similarities with these animals that if they disappeared, an important link to understanding humans would go too.

## What Is an Ecosystem?

**An ecosystem is a group of natural parts that all work together for a purpose. Ecosystems include nonliving things such as water, sunshine, and air. These are called abiotic factors. Ecosystems also include living things such as plants and animals. These are called biotic factors. The living things in an ecosystem depend on the abiotic factors in the ecosystem to survive. Every single part of the ecosystem has an important part to play. A healthy ecosystem has many different plants and animals living together. If any part of that ecosystem changes or is damaged, the other parts are affected, too.**

# ON THE MENU

Chimps eat many different foods. This helps them survive in different habitats where a wide range of food is available. Chimps eat more meat than the other **great apes**. They hunt medium-sized animals such as monkeys and small antelopes.

## FAVORITE FOODS

About half of a chimp's diet is made up of fruit. They also eat herbs, leaves, flowers, stems, and bark. Seeds, nuts, mushrooms, honey, eggs, and insects are also on the menu.

## SEARCHING FOR FOOD

Chimps have strong, long arms and grasping hands and feet. They use them to move easily through the trees. That helps them to search for food, such as fruit, leaves, and insects.

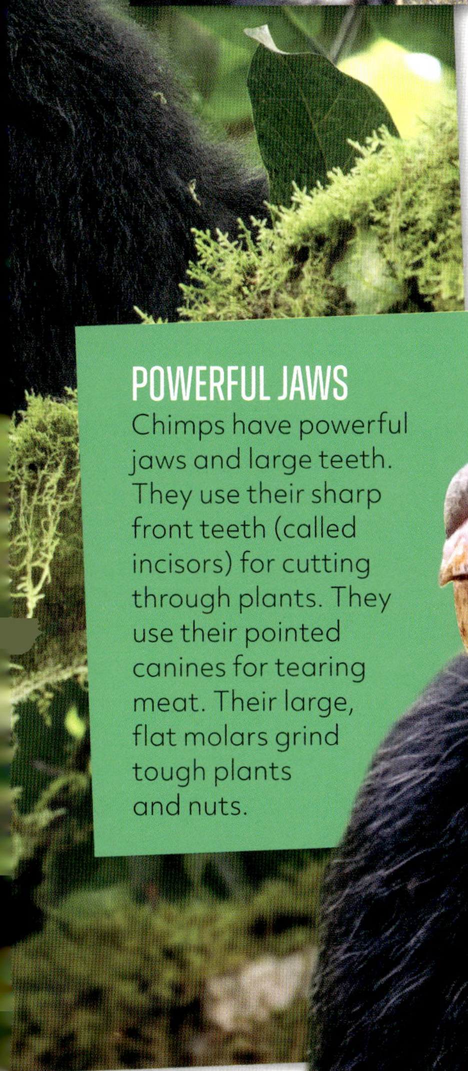

## USING TOOLS

Like humans, chimps can press their thumb against a finger to pick up and move small things. That means they can use tools to collect and prepare a wide range of foods. Chimps use stones to crack open nuts, leaves to soak up water, and sticks to catch ants.

## POWERFUL JAWS

Chimps have powerful jaws and large teeth. They use their sharp front teeth (called incisors) for cutting through plants. They use their pointed canines for tearing meat. Their large, flat molars grind tough plants and nuts.

# PEOPLE ON A MISSION

Chimps are under threat. However, many people around the world are working to save them. Some work in conservation. They have made it their mission to protect chimps. They want to secure a safe future for our closest relatives.

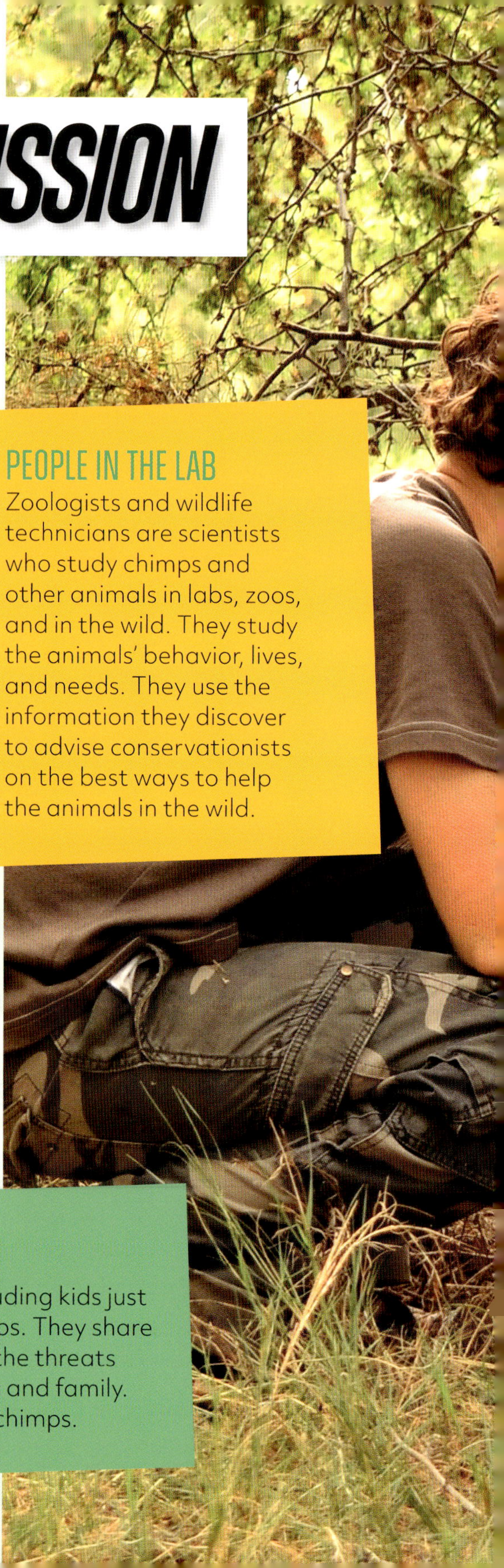

## PEOPLE IN THE LAB

Zoologists and wildlife technicians are scientists who study chimps and other animals in labs, zoos, and in the wild. They study the animals' behavior, lives, and needs. They use the information they discover to advise conservationists on the best ways to help the animals in the wild.

## PEOPLE IN OFFICES

People who work in conservation organizations use information from scientists to develop rules and guidance about conservation actions. They work with the governments in countries where chimps live. Together, they come up with plans to protect the chimps and their habitats. There are also charities in which people raise money to save chimps. Communications and public relations experts help organizations raise awareness about chimps.

## PEOPLE EVERYWHERE

Ordinary people everywhere, including kids just like you, raise money to save chimps. They share the information they learn about the threats that chimps face with their friends and family. They join organizations that help chimps.

## PEOPLE ON THE GROUND

People work in the wild to protect the chimp and its habitat. Wildlife managers, rangers, and officers are conservationists who work in places where the chimp lives. They help protect the animal's home and monitor its numbers. Wildlife technicians collect data, or information, on wildlife and habitats. Vets work to keep chimp populations healthy. Public educators and outreach specialists work with people to help educate them about chimps. They encourage people to protect chimps and make their homes a safer place in which to live.

# MAKE IT YOUR MISSION

You can help chimps and other endangered animals by taking action and planning a career in conservation. Here's how:

1. In this book, you'll discover what actions kids on a mission can take to help chimps. Use them to inspire your own actions to rescue chimps.
2. You'll also discover some of the careers people on a mission have in chimp conservation. As you read about each one, think about whether that career in conservation might suit you.
3. At the end of this book, you'll find a guide on how to build a career in conservation. Check it out to discover how you can make saving animals your life mission.

▲ Wildlife **biologists** often set up cameras to help them study animals.

CHAPTER TWO

# HOMES UNDER THREAT

Africa has one of the fastest-growing human populations in the world. The more people there are, the more land they need to live on. Unfortunately, that means less land for chimps. Chimps are forced into smaller, broken-up patches of land, which makes survival difficult.

## DESTROYING FORESTS

Local people cut and burn the forests where chimps live to clear land for homes, raising cattle, or growing food. Many local people are poor and depend on using or selling the trees for their survival. Large companies also use the land chimps live on. They clear huge areas to make space for **crops** such as cocoa and palm oil. These crops are sold to other countries. With their homes and food sources destroyed, chimps are forced to look for food on farmland. This leads to conflict with farmers.

## CUTTING DOWN HOMES

Large logging companies often cut down whole forests and sell the trees for large amounts of money. Only small patches of forest are left behind. This makes it difficult for chimps to find food, travel between important habitats, and meet with other chimps. Even when loggers take fewer trees from an area, this can damage the forest ecosystem. Many trees that are cut down are important food sources for chimps. Loggers' camps and roads disturb the chimps in remote chimp habitat. Remote places are difficult-to-reach areas far from towns and cities.

## KEEPING CHIMPS SAFE

Conservationists have set up wildlife reserves. Chimps are safe there because their habitat is protected. Wildlife reserves are monitored by people working in chimp conservation. They try and keep the chimps there safe. However, most chimps live outside wildlife reserves and are under threat from humans and more needs to be done to protect them.

◀ Chimps need forests for food, shelter, and a place to raise their young.

### Kids on a Mission

**@kelly_chimpdanger_87**

To save chimps, I have asked my family to buy products that are made only from **responsibly sourced** trees. That way, we know they are made in a way that helps protect forests and animals.

*"Preserving natural habitats is the key to conserving species. For chimpanzees, their forest homes are not just a place to live—they are essential for their survival"*

George Schaller, wildlife biologist and conservationist

# SPOTLIGHT ON FARMING

Crops such as cocoa and palm oil are grown in Africa and sold overseas. Coffee, rubber, banana, and sugarcane crops are also grown. Large areas of land are cleared to grow these crops. But that large-scale farming is a major threat to chimps because enormous areas of forest where chimps live are cleared to make space for the crops. Chimps are left without homes, food, or a safe route to other habitats.

## ATTACKING CHIMPS

Chimps depend on the forest for the plants, leaves, and fruit they eat. When chimps lose their food sources, they are forced to find food in the farmlands that have replaced the forests. When chimps take food from farmland they come into conflict with farmers, who may set traps or kill the chimps to protect their crops.

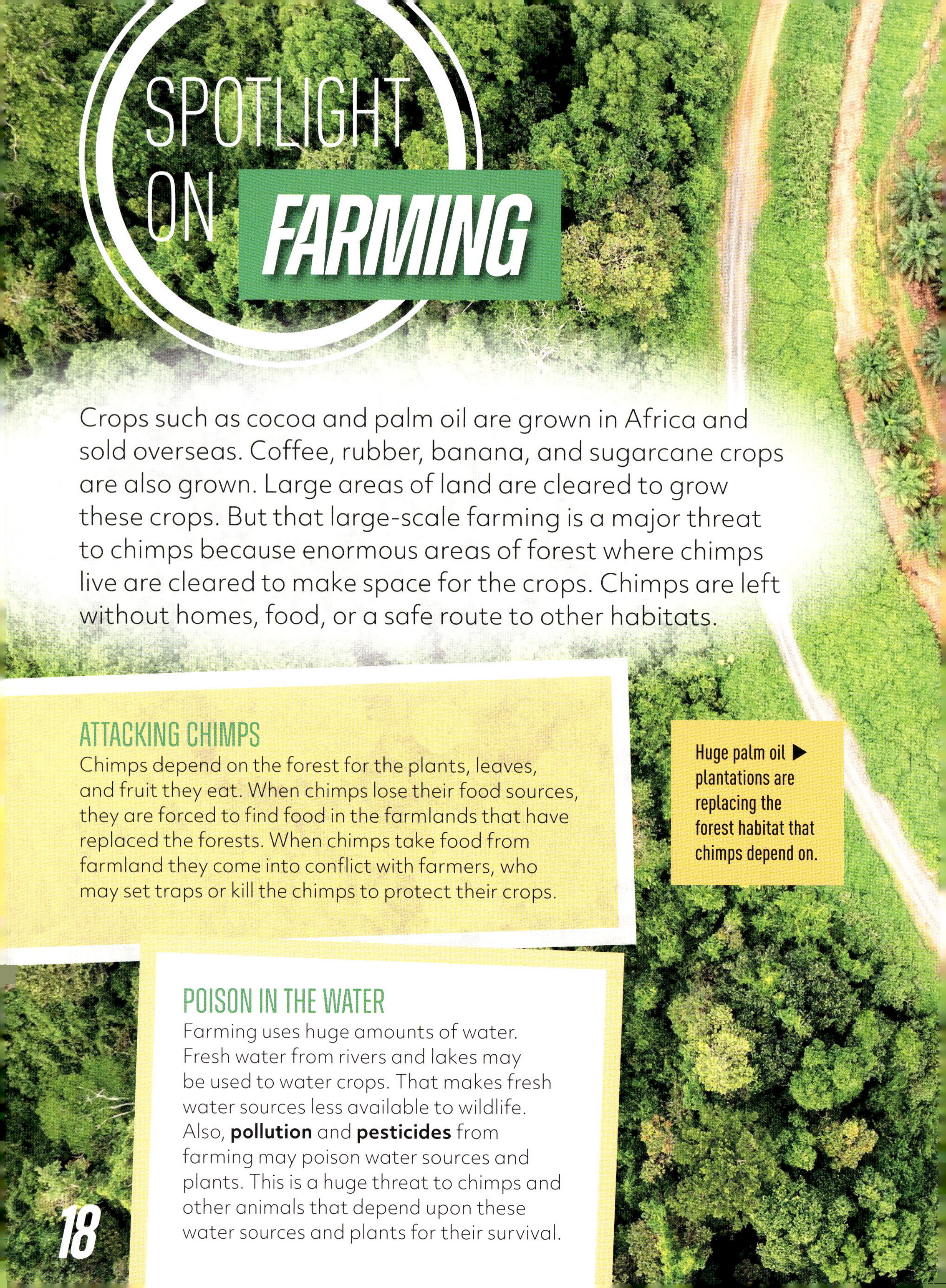

Huge palm oil ▶ plantations are replacing the forest habitat that chimps depend on.

## POISON IN THE WATER

Farming uses huge amounts of water. Fresh water from rivers and lakes may be used to water crops. That makes fresh water sources less available to wildlife. Also, **pollution** and **pesticides** from farming may poison water sources and plants. This is a huge threat to chimps and other animals that depend upon these water sources and plants for their survival.

# PEOPLE ON A MISSION: CHIMP SUPPORTERS

Specialists support farmers to plant trees to help restore forests. This is called reforestation. They are also working with local farmers to protect water sources. Wildlife policy analysts and wildlife consultants work with farmers and governments to encourage better farming practices. They include growing crops alongside trees to help wildlife such as chimps. Buffer zones are also planted with crops that chimpanzees don't like. That keeps the animals away from farms. That in turn reduces conflict between people and chimps.

Conservationists also create corridors for the chimps. These are pathways on which farmers cannot plant crops and must leave chimps alone. Wildlife corridors allow chimps to travel safely between areas to find food and mates. This helps them adapt to changes in the environment.

People working in conservation encourage farmers to take on certification from organizations, such as the Rainforest Alliance and Fair Trade. Those organizations check that farmers are working responsibly. Some farming methods are certified, or passed, as organic. That means no harmful chemicals are used during the process. Conservationists encourage farmers to use those methods. Many people want to buy food that is organic, for health reasons and to help protect the environment. Conservationists working with farmers encourage them to see the value in growing organic crops, for example, they may be able to sell them for a higher price.

Conservationists also encourage farmers to look for alternative forms of work that do not harm chimp habitats. That may include making eco-friendly crafts or ecotourism. In ecotourism, people pay to visit natural areas to see wildlife. The money helps protect the land and provides fair jobs for local people. That's a win-win for everyone, including chimps.

Around 80 percent of chimps live ▶ in unprotected areas. They are at risk from habitat loss and poaching.

# LIVING WITH THE CHIMP

Many amazing animals live alongside chimps in the **tropical** forests and savannas of Africa. Sadly, many of these animals are endangered, too.

### THE AFRICAN FOREST ELEPHANT

The African forest elephant is up to 10 feet (3 m) tall at the shoulder and weighs up to 10,000 pounds (4,500 kg). It is the smaller of the two African elephant species, with smaller ears and tusks and darker skin. These elephants live in groups in the tropical forests of west and central Africa. There, they feed on trees, shrubs, grasses, bark, leaves, and fruits. They are under threat because of habitat loss caused by logging and farming. They are also illegally hunted for their **ivory tusks**.

## THE OKAPI

The okapi is often called the "forest giraffe." That is because it is the giraffe's only living relative. Like the giraffe, the okapi has large ears and a long tongue, which it uses to strip leaves and bark from branches. It has a shorter neck than a giraffe and a velvety dark coat. It has black-and-white stripes on its legs, like a zebra. The stripes help the okapi blend into the dappled light of its forest habitat. The okapi is under threat from habitat loss, hunting, and fighting among different **militant** groups.

## THE PYGMY HIPPO

The pygmy hippo lives alone or in small family groups in the thick, swampy forests of west Africa. At only 3 feet (1m) tall, 5 feet (1.5m) long, and 600 pounds (70 kg), the pygmy hippo is the smallest hippo. These shy hippos spend the day hiding and swimming in rivers, streams, and swamps. They feed on land at night, eating fruit, leaves, and plants. Sadly, these gentle animals are under threat too. That is because their forest habitat is being cleared for rubber, coffee, and oil palm farms. Only small patches of forest are left for the hippos. They are also threatened by mining and hunting.

CHAPTER THREE

# UNDER THREAT FROM POACHING

Poaching is the illegal killing or capture of animals. Poachers kill chimps for their meat. Bushmeat is meat from wild animals. Poachers also sell baby chimps as pets. Although this is illegal, some people risk being caught because poaching is their only source of food or money.

## RAIN FOREST ROADS

In the past, it was difficult for poachers to reach remote areas of forest where chimps lived. Now, chimp habitat is crisscrossed with roads built by logging companies. Poachers use these roads to quickly reach chimp habitat. This has made poaching a much greater threat for chimps.

## THE WILDLIFE TRADE

When poachers kill chimp mothers, they may take the babies and sell them as pets. Some are sold to circuses, zoos, or for use in movies and television. Criminals **smuggle** the babies to other countries. Many of these babies die of stress, hunger, and disease. Some organizations rescue the baby chimps and care for them.

## MANY DIFFERENT REASONS

Bushmeat is a traditional food in parts of Africa. People rely on bushmeat to feed their families. Bushmeat is also sold at markets. In areas far from towns and cities, there are often few jobs. There, selling bushmeat is one way people can make money. Chimp body parts are sold as trophies. Trophies are things that are prized by people. The body parts of the animals are also sold for use in traditional medicine.

◀ Chimp babies are often taken by poachers who sell them as pets in the illegal wildlife trade.

## Kids on a Mission

**@joe_chimpssneedus_001**

I asked to **adopt** a chimp for my birthday. The charity I adopted through cares for baby chimps rescued from the illegal pet trade. It feels good to know the chimps have a safe home now.

*"Every chimpanzee lost to poaching is a tragic loss to our world. These magnificent creatures are disappearing, and it's up to us to stop the cycle of destruction."*

Paulette McCann, founder of Wildlife Conservation Efforts

# SPOTLIGHT ON BUSHMEAT

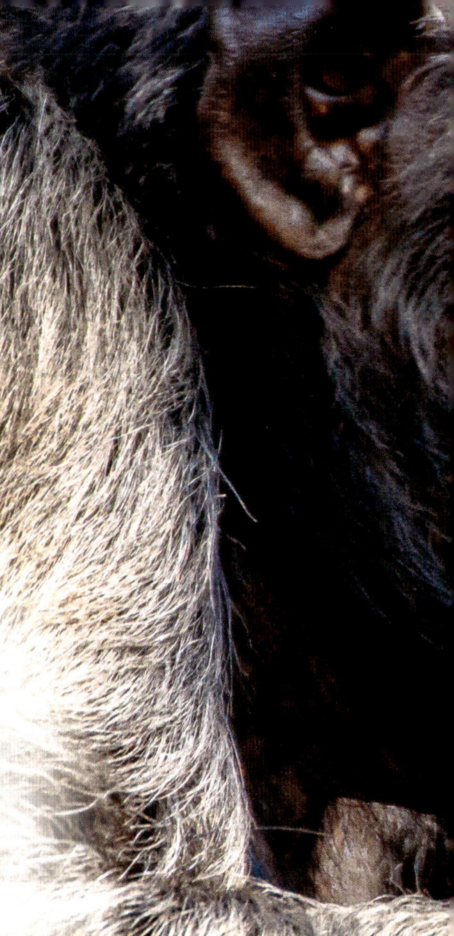

The trade in bushmeat takes place throughout west and central Africa. It is one of the biggest threats facing chimps today. In the past, local people caught only the food they needed to survive. Today, there is more demand for bushmeat. It is sold to workers in logging camps and mines. It is sometimes sold in towns and cities as a luxury food, which is even sold to other countries. Criminal gangs poach and sell bushmeat on a large scale. This means that many chimps are killed for the bushmeat trade.

▼ Rangers patrol protected areas and keep chimps safe from poachers.

## DEADLY TO CHIMPS

Killing chimps for bushmeat is devastating to chimp populations. Chimps reproduce slowly, so it can take many years for a chimp group to recover from poaching. Chimps take many years to grow to adulthood. Poachers target adult chimps. Without older chimps to teach them, young chimps can't learn the important skills they need to survive. If a chimp mom is killed, her baby may die without the care it needs.

◀ When poachers kill older chimps, young chimps lose their chance to learn the precious skills they need to survive.

## PEOPLE ON A MISSION: CHIMP PROTECTORS

Wildlife rangers work in different ways to protect the chimp and prevent poaching for bushmeat. They patrol large areas of land where chimps are protected. They watch out for illegal activities and track and stop poachers. They have the power to arrest them and can take away any bushmeat and weapons the poachers may have.

Wildlife rangers also work to create stronger **boundaries** around protected areas to keep poachers from getting in. They cut or clear away wire snare animal traps that they find. They also save injured chimps. They monitor the chimps' health and collect vital conservation data.

Rangers talk to local people about why hunting for bushmeat is so harmful to chimps. They educate local children who could one day be tempted to hunt for bushmeat, too. They discuss things that local people could do instead to earn money. They try and help them find alternatives to eating wild bushmeat, such as wild meat from **sustainable** hunting or the **domestication** of wild animals.

# CHIMP BABIES

A female chimp gives birth to three to four babies over her entire lifetime. Only half of those babies will make it to adulthood. This low rate of **reproduction** makes it difficult for chimp populations to recover if chimps are killed.

### CHIMP MOMS

A chimp is pregnant for around seven to eight months before she gives birth. Like humans, female chimps usually give birth to one baby at a time. They may sometimes have twins. Chimp babies weigh about 3.5 pounds (1.6 kg) at birth—about the same weight as a loaf of bread.

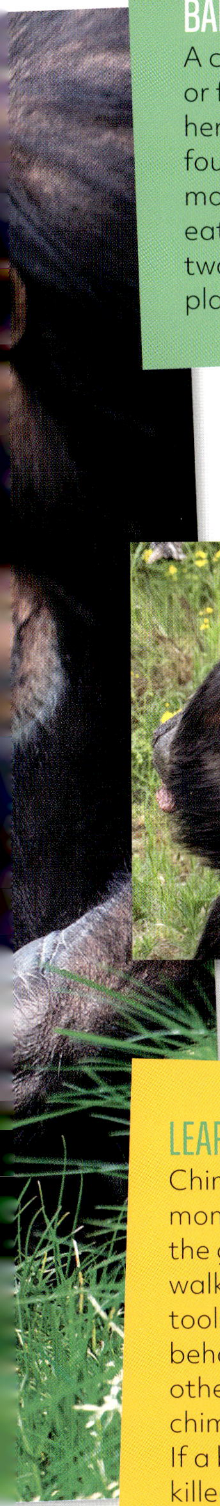

## BABY FOOD

A chimp mom nurses her baby, or feeds it with milk from her body, until it is three to four years old. At around six months old, the baby starts eating some plants. By one to two years old, it eats mostly plants, leaves, and insects.

## KEEPING CLOSE

A chimp baby is helpless, like a human baby. A chimp mom carries her baby for the first few months. As it gets older, the baby clings to mom's belly with its hands and feet. It later rides on her back. The baby stays close to its mom for four to five years. It depends on her for care, food, warmth, and safety.

## LEARNING TO SURVIVE

Chimps learn by copying their moms and other chimps in the group. They learn how to walk, climb, find food, and use tools. They also learn how to behave and communicate with other chimps. These skills help chimps to survive as adults. If a baby chimp's mother is killed, the baby won't learn the skills it needs to survive.

CHAPTER FOUR

# THE THREAT OF CLIMATE CHANGE

Climate change is having a dangerous impact on habitats, humans, and wildlife. It is causing rising temperatures and changes in weather patterns. That damages the forests in which chimps live. That makes it harder for chimps to find the food, water, and shelter they need to survive.

## WHAT IS CLIMATE CHANGE?

Climate change is a change in temperature or weather in an area over a period of time. Climate change has always happened slowly throughout Earth's history, due to natural factors such as changes in the sun and geological activity. However, the climate change we are experiencing today is largely caused by human activities. These include burning fossil fuels, which releases gases into Earth's atmosphere. The gases circle the planet like a blanket, making it heat up.

◀ Cars release harmful gases that are contributing to climate change.

## THREATS FROM HEAT, STORMS, DROUGHTS, AND FLOODS

Climate change is causing temperatures to rise across the planet. It is heating up the forests where chimps live. That is making some of the forests too hot for chimps. Extreme heat can make chimps sick. Climate change also changes rainfall patterns. Heavy rains that cause floods damage the forest and pollute water sources. In other areas, there are long periods of dry weather when it hardly rains, called droughts. In a drought, rivers and streams dry up, making it difficult for chimps to find drinking water. Plants and trees that chimps depend on for food and shelter are damaged by flooding and drought. Animals chimps depend on for food may also die.

◀ Climate change is making storms stronger and damaging forest habitats.

### Kids on a Mission

**@lily_savechimps_257**

My friends and I are trying to help stop climate change. We bicycle to school instead of going by car. We're helping to save the planet and getting healthy, too.

*"Climate change is one of the biggest threats facing chimpanzees. ...their habitats are shrinking, making it harder for them to find food and shelter."*

Jane Goodall, primatologist and conservationist

# SPOTLIGHT ON FLOODING AND DROUGHTS

Chimps rely on their forest habitat. Changes to those forests could make it difficult for chimps to survive. Plants and animals need water to survive. During a drought, many of the animals and plants that chimps depend on for food may die.

## DEADLY DROUGHTS

Many of the trees that chimps depend on for food need regular rainfall to keep their leaves healthy and produce fruit. During a drought, those trees may stop producing fruit and their leaves may dry up. If the drought continues, even the trees may die.

## SHRINKING HABITATS

As climate change makes chimps' forest homes less suitable, chimps are forced to travel farther for food, water, and shelter. They are forced to compete for resources with humans and other animals. Resources are things that people and animals need, such as food and water.

▲ Flooding damages the plants and trees chimps depend on for food and shelter. It also pollutes their sources of drinking water.

## PEOPLE ON A MISSION: FIGHTING CLIMATE CHANGE

Many people are working hard to help chimps survive climate change. Scientists are studying how climate change is affecting chimps and their forest homes. They are monitoring how changes in temperature and rainfall affect chimps' behavior, health, and food sources. One big worry is how rising temperatures and changing rainfall patterns might harm the forests where chimps live. As the climate changes, some trees and plants may not grow as well. This may lead to food shortages for chimps and make it harder for them to survive.

To help, people are replanting trees in damaged forests. Planting trees and improving forest health helps provide chimps with the food and shelter they need. People are also working to make ecosystems more diverse. Diverse means to have many different types of plants and animals. A forest with more types of plants and animals can better survive climate change.

As climate change alters ecosystems, some forests that once provided food and shelter for chimps may become impossible to live in. When that happens, chimps need to find new places to live. As chimps look for new homes, they can face dangers such as having to cross roads with busy traffic. They are more likely to experience conflict with humans too. That is why it is essential to build wildlife corridors for chimps—they need them to safely move between different forests so they can find new homes.

◀ Chimps depend on forest trees for fruit.

# CHIMPS NEED FORESTS

Chimps are adapted to the forests and savanna woodlands of Africa. That means their bodies and behavior have changed to suit the environment in which they live. They rely on their environment for food, shelter, and safety.

### FOOD AND WATER

Chimps can eat a variety of forest foods. They feed on what is available at the time. To find enough to eat, chimps need large areas of forest in which to look for different foods. They also need clean rivers, streams, and ponds for their drinking water.

## SHELTER AND SAFETY

Chimps spend most of their time in trees. This protects them from animals that hunt them, such as leopards and lions. Every evening, chimps bend branches and leaves to make a nest in the trees. They sleep in the nest. Chimps need large, strong trees in which to build these nests. The overhead leaves and branches of the trees protect the animals from the sun, rain, and cold.

## CHIMPS NEED SPACE

Chimps live in large groups that need plenty of space. Living in large groups helps chimps make friends and find **mates**. Chimps are intelligent. They also need space to explore and learn about different types of land, trees, and water sources.

## LIFE IN THE TREES

Chimps are perfectly adapted for treetop living. Their muscular bodies and grasping hands and feet help them climb and swing through trees. Chimps have amazing balance. They can move easily between branches without falling.

CHAPTER FIVE

# OTHER THREATS TO CHIMPS

Climate change and habitat loss are major threats for chimps. So too are poaching, logging, and farming. Sadly, these amazing apes face other threats, too.

## GETTING SICK

Chimps can easily catch diseases from people. The more people encounter chimps, the more the animals are exposed to human diseases. Like humans, chimps can catch colds and the flu from coughs, sneezes, and human touch. They can also catch diseases from resting, drinking, and feeding in areas that contain human waste such as urine and feces.

As people's homes and farms are built closer to chimp habitats, the risk of chimps catching human diseases from **contaminated** land or water sources increases. Poachers, loggers, and miners may carry diseases into chimp habitats. Even researchers and tourists who get close to chimps may pass on deadly diseases to the animals.

### Kids on a Mission

**@ben_chimprescue_101**

I did a sponsored run to raise money for the World Wildlife Fund (WWF). They teach local people and tourists how to stop chimps catching human diseases.

"Chimpanzees are facing a new danger: diseases that humans bring into their environments. As their habitats shrink and they come into more contact with humans, these risks are growing."

Frans de Waal, primatologist

▼ People love to see chimps in the wild. However, tourism can put chimps at risk of catching diseases.

## WAR AND CONFLICT

Armed groups fighting to control valuable mines are a threat to chimps and their habitats. During fighting, it can become too dangerous for conservationists to work in an area. Military roads, camps, and people running away to escape war often take over chimp habitat. That leads to more poaching and the spread of diseases.

## THE THREAT OF MINING

Mining is a growing threat to chimps. People clear large areas of forest to mine for gold, diamonds, oil, and minerals. Mining uses chemicals that pollute the food and water sources of chimps. Workers and noise from machinery can scare the chimps. Increased contact with workers also puts chimps at greater risk of poaching, disease, and conflict.

# SPOTLIGHT ON DISEASE

Since chimps live in remote places, human diseases are new to them. That means their bodies have not learned how to fight these diseases. Illnesses like the flu or common cold are mild for humans but can cause serious illness or death in chimpanzees.

## DEADLY DISEASE

Ebola is a major threat to chimps, causing many deaths in the wild. The **virus** affects both humans and chimps, and some outbreaks of the disease have killed up to 90 percent of the chimp population. Chimps are especially at risk because the virus spreads quickly in forests where they live. Stress from habitat loss and poaching also makes chimps' bodies weaker, and less able to fight diseases. Ebola outbreaks have greatly reduced chimpanzee numbers, especially in central Africa.

▼ In 1994, an Ebola outbreak killed about 90 percent of the chimp population in Taï National Park.

▼ Just as diseases spread quickly from human to chimp, they spread quickly between chimps too.

## PEOPLE ON A MISSION: CHIMP SCIENTISTS

Scientists and zoologists are on a mission to protect chimps from Ebola. First, they make sure to avoid contact with wild chimps. When scientists do need to interact with chimps, they wear protective gear and clean everything they carry to prevent passing diseases from humans to chimps.

Protecting chimp habitats is another important step. By stopping the clearing of forest land and limiting human activity in chimp habitats, chimps are less likely to come into contact with humans. This helps reduce the risk of disease. Scientists work with local communities to teach people about the dangers of Ebola. They teach people not to come into close contact with chimps. While there isn't yet a **vaccine** for chimps, researchers are testing vaccines that could help both humans and animals in the future.

Scientists also monitor chimp populations for signs of the disease. By tracking both human and animal health, they can spot outbreaks early and stop them from spreading. If an Ebola outbreak does happen, scientists quickly contain the infected chimps and do everything they can to stop the virus from spreading. These efforts are helping to protect chimps and prevent Ebola from causing more harm.

# OTHER GREAT APES IN DANGER

Chimps are not the only great apes under threat. Around the world, other great apes face similar dangers. They are also rapidly losing much of their forest habitat to farming, logging, and mining.

## THE GORILLA

Gorillas live in the faraway forests of west, central, and east Africa. They are found in high montane rain forests and bamboo forests. They also live in lowland rain forests and swamp forests. Gorillas are known as "gentle giants." This is because although they are the largest and strongest of the apes, they are generally very calm and peaceful. Gorillas live mostly on the forest floor, in large groups. They can walk upright but mostly walk on all fours. They eat leaves, roots, fruit, and tree bark. Habitat loss, poaching, and disease are major threats to the gorilla.

## THE ORANGUTAN

Orangutans live in the rain forests of Borneo and Sumatra, in Southeast Asia. The orangutan is the only great ape found outside of Africa. These red-haired apes spend most of their time in the trees. Their long, powerful arms and grasping hands and feet help them swing through the trees. Orangutans are highly intelligent. They use tools to catch insects and prepare the fruit that they eat. They also build sleeping platforms in the trees every night from branches and leaves. These amazing apes are under threat from habitat loss and hunting.

## THE BONOBO

The bonobo lives in rain forests in the Democratic Republic of the Congo (DRC), in central Africa. Bonobos are similar to chimps. However, they have smaller bodies and ears, but larger eyes. They often walk upright, just like humans. Bonobos are very intelligent. They are more peaceful than chimps and live in groups led by females.

# WHAT'S NEXT FOR THE CHIMP?

The future of chimps depends on how well we protect them from the serious threats they face. But there is hope for the chimp. Many ordinary people, conservationists, and governments are working hard to protect this amazing animal.

## HELP FROM CONSERVATIONISTS

Conservationists are working with local people to protect chimps. They help find ways for people to earn money without harming the environment, for example, by working in ecotourism or farming in a way that does not harm chimp habitats. When local people are educated about chimps, poaching for bushmeat lessens.

Conservationists also involve local people in monitoring and protecting the chimps from poachers. They also work with governments to make stronger laws that protect chimps. By working with local people, conservationists make sure both chimps and people can thrive.

@jen_chimpSOS_now1

I'm working hard in my science subjects. I want to be a zoologist one day, so I can work with chimps and help to save them.

> "The future for chimpanzees is fragile, but it's not too late. If we take action now, we can prevent their extinction and secure a future for them in the wild."
>
> Biruté Galdikas, primatologist

## HELP FROM ORGANIZATIONS

Several organizations are fighting to save chimps. The WWF protects chimp habitats by creating protected areas. They work with governments to stop illegal logging, mining, and poaching in chimp habitat. The Jane Goodall Institute and the Pan African Sanctuary Alliance (PASA) rescue and care for chimps that have lost their mothers. They help them recover in safe sanctuaries. The Born Free Foundation and PASA fight poaching by training park rangers and helping stop illegal wildlife trade. These groups also work with local communities, teaching people how to protect chimps and their habitats. Research on chimps helps these organizations better understand the animals' needs and plan conservation actions.

## HELP FROM ALL OF US

We can all help save the chimp. We can live, travel, eat, and shop in more sustainable ways to reduce the threat of climate change. We can learn more about threats to chimps, so that we can raise awareness of the issues. By working together, it is possible to save these animals. About 20 percent of chimps now live in protected areas. In places where local people work in ecotourism and farm sustainably, there is less poaching and clearing of forests. If we all work together, we can save the world's chimps.

# MAKE IT YOUR MISSION: A CAREER IN CONSERVATION

▲ Take your first step toward a career in conservation by working hard in your science class.

Why not make it your mission to build a future career in conservation? That way, you could make a huge difference to chimps and other endangered animals. On pages 44–45 you'll find some of the conservation careers you could pursue. And here are things you can do right now to prepare for a career in conservation and help save chimps.

## GET SET TO STUDY

Working hard at school now will pay off if you want a conservation career. Pay attention in your science, English, and geography classes. Languages are also useful. If you have a job oversees, being able to speak a foreign language is helpful.

## GET CONNECTED

Connecting with other people who care about wildlife is a great way to feel empowered about saving endangered animals. You'll find some organizations you can join on page 47. By connecting with other people who are concerned about the environment, you'll find out what you can do to help. Being involved with conservation organizations and charities now will also help you when you apply for jobs in the future. It will show that you have been interested in conservation from an early age.

# TAKE ACTION!

You have learned about some of the actions that help chimps from the Kids on a Mission features in this book. Here are some more ideas for other activities that can help protect chimps:

- A mineral called coltan is used to make cell phones. Mining for it can harm chimp habitats. Avoid updating your cell phone too often. Recycle it to reduce the impact of coltan mining.
- Ask your parents to buy furniture and wooden items that are FSC certified. This means that the wood comes from forests that are sustainably managed.
- Adopt a chimp! Ask your parents to help you check out the WWF site for information about adopting chimps.
- Choose FSC-certified or recycled tissue and toilet paper. These products are not made from paper from trees cut down in rain forests.
- Ask your school to hold a fundraising event to raise money for an organization such as WWF to help them protect chimps.
- Start a blog about chimps and the dangers they face. Educate as many people as you can.

## GET EXPERIENCE

Any form of work experience in wildlife care will be useful for a future conservation career. Why not apply to local zoos, charities, and conservation organizations as soon as you are old enough?

Adopting a chimp is a great ▶ way to help protect the animal and its species.

# CAREERS IN CONSERVATION

If you care about the future of chimps and other endangered animals, why not make protecting them your mission? You could do that by planning for a future career in conservation. There are many conservation jobs available. Here is information about just some of them. You can find out about other conservation jobs on page 47 of this book.

▲ This guide is leading tourists through the rain forest in the Congo, in central Africa.

## WILDLIFE CONSERVATIONIST

Wildlife conservationists work with and care for a variety of wild animals. In this role you would monitor animals to collect data for conservation records that help improve our understanding of wildlife. You might also care for animals directly, ensuring that they are healthy and well. This varied job could take you all over the world. A degree in wildlife management is often required.

## MAPPING CONSERVATIONIST

Making maps of animal habitats and how they are changing provides vital information for conservationists. The job is quite varied. For example, in this role, you could produce a map to show the location of a newly discovered species. You could also work through data to map areas where another species is most often found. If you enjoy mapping and computers, this could be the conservation career path for you.

## FIELD GUIDE

Field guides are wildlife experts. If you became one, you would guide people through natural habitats and educate them about the wildlife living there. You might take people to see wildlife in a vehicle or on foot. Field guides must understand animal behavior and tracking. Many field guides work in ecotourism. In this industry, visitors pay to see wildlife, which helps conserve their habitats.

## PUBLIC RELATIONS OFFICER

Public relations officers who work in conservation have the job of raising awareness about issues that affect wild habitats and the animals that live in them. They may work for charities, wildlife organizations, or governments. They run campaigns to make people aware of wildlife issues. They read complicated reports and then explain them to organizations and the public. If you are a good communicator, this could be an ideal job for you. A degree in marketing would be useful for this role.

◀ As a wildlife photographer or filmmaker, your job would be to capture animals in their natural environment on film.

## CONSERVATION PHOTOGRAPHER OR FILMMAKER

Photos and videos of wild animals and the beautiful, threatened places where they live are hugely important to conservation. They can inspire people to care about wildlife and do something to help animals in danger. Wildlife images may feature in magazine or newspaper campaigns. The images may also become part of a television series. Wildlife photography and filmmaking are popular and competitive conservation careers. To work in this field, you will need to practice your photography or filmmaking to make sure you are highly skilled. You will also need to educate yourself about wildlife and the habitats you photograph or film. Studying photography and film are essential.

# GLOSSARY

**adopt** to take on part of the responsibility for the safety and wellbeing of an animal
**biologists** scientists who study biology
**boundaries** the edges of something
**communicate** to share messages or information
**conservation** protection of the planet
**conservationists** people who try to protect the planet
**contaminated** contains something dangerous
**critically endangered** facing an extremely high risk of extinction in the wild
**crops** plants grown for food
**digestive system** part of the body in which food is broken down and used
**DNA** short for Deoxyribonucleic acid. DNA is material that carries the codes for how a living thing will look and behave
**domestication** the process of turning something wild into something tame
**endangered** facing a high risk of extinction in the wild
**expressive** easily shows emotions
**facial expressions** movements of the face to show emotions
**gestures** movements of the hands and head in order to communicate
**great apes** large primates that include chimps, gorillas, bonobos, and orangutans
**habitat** the place in which a plant or animal lives
**humid** hot and wet
**ivory tusks** long teeth found on animals such as elephants
**lowland forests** areas of forest on the lower slopes of mountains
**manipulate** to bend and shape as required
**mates** comes together with a member of the opposite sex to reproduce
**militant** related to the military, or army
**mining** the extraction, or taking out, of minerals from the ground
**montane forests** areas of trees that are found above the lowlands of a mountain but before its upper reaches
**oil palm plantations** farms in which oil palms are grown
**opposable** can move to touch other fingers, helping with gripping
**pesticides** chemicals sprayed onto plants to kill insects that feed on them
**poaching** the illegal killing of an animal
**pollution** harmful substances that make something dirty or dangerous to touch, eat, or drink
**population** all the members of a species living in a certain area
**preserving** keeping alive and healthy
**primatologist** a scientist who studies primates, a group of animals that includes chimps
**rain forests** forests that receive a lot of rain and that are often found in tropical areas
**relatives** living things that are related to each other, or share DNA
**reproduction** the process of creating young
**responsibly sourced** taken in a way that does not harm the environment
**savanna woodlands** areas that are a mix of trees and grassland
**smuggle** to illegally transport something from one country to another
**subspecies** a group that is ranked, or ordered, just below the main species group
**sustainable** can be relied upon for the foreseeable future
**swamp forests** areas of trees that are found in swampy ground, or land that is mainly covered with shallow fresh water
**tropical** near the tropics, which are areas near an imaginary line around the planet known as the equator
**vaccine** a substance that is often injected into a living thing in order to protect it against a disease
**virus** a tiny organism that has the ability to infect other organisms with disease

# FIND OUT MORE

## BOOKS

Gagne, Tammy. *Endangered Mammals* (Focus on Endangered Species). ReferencePoint Press, 2024.

Jenkins, Martin. *Endangered Animals*. Walker Studio, 2024.

Spilsbury, Louise. *Saving the Gorilla* (Mission Survival: Saving Earth's Endangered Animals). Cheriton Children's Books, 2023.

Spilsbury, Louise. *Saving the Orangutan* (Mission Survival: Saving Earth's Endangered Animals). Cheriton Children's Books, 2023.

## WEBSITES

Discover more about careers that help fight climate change at:
**www.bestcolleges.com/blog/climate-change-jobs**

Hear directly from people working in conservation! Find out what they have to say about working in a career in conservation at:
**www.conservation-careers.com/conservation-jobs-careers-advice/how-to-get-a-job-in-conservation**

Discover the ultimate guide to careers in conservation at:
**www.conservation-careers.com/15-key-conservation-jobs-ultimate-guide-for-conservation-job-seekers**

Find out more about chimps at the Jane Goodall Institute site:
**https://janegoodall.org**

Discover careers in environmental science at:
**https://jobs.environmentalscience.org**

**Publisher's note to educators and parents:**
All the websites featured above have been carefully reviewed to ensure that they are suitable for students. However, many websites change often, and we cannot guarantee that a site's future contents will continue to meet our high standards of educational value. Please be advised that students should be closely monitored whenever they access the Internet.

# INDEX



## ABOUT THE AUTHOR

Katherine Eason has written many books about the natural world. She is passionate about conservation, and hopes this book inspires readers to make it their mission to help save the chimp.